Shipping Container Homes

The complete guide to building shipping container homes, including plans, FAQS, cool ideas, and more!

Table of Contents

Introduction

Thank you for taking the time to read this book: Shipping Container Homes.

This book covers the topic of shipping container homes, and will help you to build your own! This book serves as an introductory guide to shipping container homes, what they are, how they can be made, and why you should build one!

You will soon discover the different benefits of having a shipping container home, including the incredible cost-savings that can be had.

At the completion of this book you will have a good understanding of the different things that you can do with shipping container homes, and feel confident in building your own! You will have a list of actionable steps to take to firstly prepare yourself for building a container home, then hiring people to create plans and acquire permits, and finally complete the actual build.

Within a time period of several weeks to a few months you could have a fully built shipping container home of your own!

Once again, thanks for picking up this book, I hope you find it to be helpful!

Chapter 1:
What You Should Know About Shipping Container Homes

There are different kinds of homes available these days varying on structural design, materials used, and the overall dimensions employed. Usually, homeowners choose a style of house based on personal design preferences, sustainability, and of course, their budget.

There are certain types of homes which are more expensive to construct than others and oftentimes require a larger parcel of land to be constructed on. Some allow for a DIY approach while others call for no less than a professional team of workers from contractors to architects to landscapers.

With housing markets currently in a volatile state and with home prices rising every passing year, people who are interested in home ownership rather than rentals are becoming more innovative in their choice of shelter.

One mode of housing that is increasingly becoming popular makes use of shipping containers for its base structure. Indeed, shipping container homes have grown to become a more affordable, cost-effective, sustainable, and unique form of housing.

Different countries across continents regularly make use of shipping containers to satisfy their importation and exportation needs. These cargo units are built from reinforced steel allowing them to function despite exposure to harsh weather conditions and heavy loads not to mention rough handling across ports.

These are used to transport various products on land, sea, and air. To satisfy their primary purpose, they are manufactured in such a way that durability is never an issue thereby making them excellent structures for makeshift houses.

Thousands, if not millions of these containers are regularly manufactured every year to cater to a growing demand. Homeowners interested in having a shipping container to build a home with can either buy them new or second hand.

Regardless of their quality, these are always available to those who need them and the price tag for a pre-fabricated structure is relatively cheap compared to having to build one from scratch when constructing a house.

Not only is the cost rather enticing but using these containers make for a greener approach to homebuilding as well. When old units are bought for the purpose of building a house, the steel is recycled without having to exert additional effort or cost in the recycling process. It significantly reduces one's carbon footprint adding to its appeal for new age homeowners.

Although the space a shipping container provides can be quite limited, it has the feature of being open to modifications. A comfortable house can easily be made by combining several of these containers vertically or horizontally.

Homeowners who can survive without that much space can even build a house from a single unit without much hassle. Because the structure has already been pre-fabricated, builders who love to do the job themselves, provided that they are skilled handymen, have the ability to construct container homes without the need for professional assistance, further dropping their construction costs.

There are more features of shipping container homes than what the eyes can see. They have their fair share of pros and cons. Different elements go into the construction process. Various costs come with this type of project and so on and so forth.

Reading on, you will find out more about these container units, how they function, and how they can readily be used to create a one-of-a-kind home. You will also learn important steps and guidelines that will help you build a shipping container home, properly enabling you to save on costs and preventing the onset of structural problems as time passes.

These days, sustainability is a very important concept that many have begun to embrace. Resource conservation can come in the form of energy saving lights like LEDs or through the use of recycled materials for varying purposes including construction. This is where intermodal shipping units enter the picture.

Although shipping container homes can be built using new containers, most homeowners choose to purchase used containers for their projects. By not having to manufacture additional steel cargo units for residential purposes, there is an immediate conservation of resources and energy. This means that aside from the reduction in carbon emissions during the build and use of shipping container homes, there can also be a reduction in embodied carbon emissions.

Shipping container homes can be connected to power grids but their transportability allows homeowners to live off of the grid. The use of solar panel installations are quite popular in this type of residential endeavor. Aside from being able to save money on electricity and other utility expenses, homeowners can also live in an environmentally friendly fashion.

Shipping container homes provide an alternative residential option that also opens doors to the conservation of everything from timber to the local landscape.

It also helps protect water streams by controlling daily pollution. Traditional construction processes are responsible for a huge amount of the world's total air, noise, and water pollutants.

Chapter 2:
What Are Shipping Containers?

There are three main purposes that shipping containers serve to satisfy. They are meant to withstand heavy loads of shipment, product storage, and excessive handling without much of a hassle. It is with these reasons in mind that these cargo containers are built to last; to be as strong and durable as possible so as not to succumb to wear and tear early in their life. There are different types of shipping containers and these come in varying sizes as well.

Most common are the steel boxes that can be used over and over again, and then there are those that are meant for short term reliability, the corrugated boxes. The former is utilized for what is known as intermodal shipping. It basically means that the container has been designed to be moved or transported from one location to another without having to be unloaded, not to mention repacked.

The most common type of container used for shipping container homes are the intermodal freight shipping containers. Aside from domestic transport, other locational transport needs for various products including those done from country to country are satisfied by intermodal freight shipping containers.

There are millions of these cargo units around the world, some of which are in active transit, others stored in warehouses, and others reused in various ways. When it comes to long-distance freight done on a global scale, these shipping containers play very important roles. Although these are extremely dependable, sending them back to their points of origin can be costly.

It is cheaper to simply source new ones should the need for such a container arise. This is why most of these intermodal containers are discarded, to save costs on the return trip. The improvement of intercontinental trade can be attributed to the invention of these cargo containers. Not only have they been able to help reduce transport costs but they also helped prevent losses from product damage.

When it comes to the fabrication of these intermodal shipping containers, they are known for being highly durable with the most popular variety being those made out of heavy duty steel. There is always the question of why these boxes are so strong and what makes them such and the answer is simple.

These cargo units are extremely strong because of the metal composite that they have been fabricated from. Because they are designed to withstand the elements not to mention heavy loads, and because they are meant to be used and reused over time, a special kind of steel material, Corten, is used.

Corten is a type of steel component often referred to as weathering steel. The material, when exposed to the elements, allows light rust to form on the surface. To most, this might not seem to be the best thing but the light rust actually acts as a secondary barrier or armor which strengthens the steel over time. The rust does not progress to the degree which eats at the metal.

In this case, it is more of an ally to the steel rather than an enemy. Aside from shipping containers, this material is also used to reinforce bridges, towers, chimneys, sculptures, and rail cars to name a few. Every time a shipping container is made, manufacturers line the Corten walls with marine grade paint which acts as a sealant and protective coating. Over time, the paint will degrade due to wear and tear. It is during this time that the material starts promulgating the formation of light rust which replaces the paint as the structure's external protection.

Intermodal shipping containers are some of the most widely used cargo units around the world. These are made out of a steel composite and come in various types not to mention sizes. A huge chunk of the total number of available shipping containers around the globe are referred to as dry freight which basically means that they are general purpose containers used to transport different dry materials or products across continents.

These durable steel boxes come with double ended doors which can be closed and sealed with ease. The standard lengths are either twenty or forty feet with a height ranging from eight and a half to nine and a half feet. If necessary, an extender can be added to the top wall, offering an additional foot of height per container.

An intermodal shipping container is one of the larger shipping boxes readily available today and is designed to cater to intermodal transport. It means that these boxes can be shipped via different modes of transportation including land, air, and sea.

Aside from this, the containers can be shipped without having to unload or reload cargo until they reach their final destination. Securing the boxes is easy as there are multiple locking systems in each one with the final keys only available to the shipper or receiver.

Similar to how pallets and cardboard boxes function, these kinds of shipping containers are ideal for bundling cargo into an easy-to-handle package. The containers can easily be moved using lifters or cranes, they can neatly be placed side by side, and they can also be stacked atop one another.

Aside from easy transport, this also allows for organized storage. All of these capabilities, together with the individual identifying marks and details per container unit, can be attributed to several key construction features applied to these shipping containers.

Millions of these intermodal cargo units can be found around the world actively being used in the constant importation and exportation of goods and materials. Years after their inception, they have become the primary choice for carrying cargo as they allow for more effective and efficient transport.

For a twenty footer, it weighs an average of 2200 kg empty and can handle a content load of 28200 kg for a final net allowable load of 30400 kg. The forty footer can handle the same net weight but weighs more when empty, around 3800 kg which means the maximum internal load it can handle is about 26600 kg.

In the case of stacking, without additional support pillars, standard forty footers can be stacked one on top of the other. Without modifications, it is not safe to stack containers of differing size on top of one another.

For twenty footers, they can only hold a second storey forty footer if there are two twenty footers side by side supporting the load. It is always best to consult a structural engineer when it comes to something like this to ensure that the structure is balanced and safe for whatever purpose it intends to serve.

It was during the 1940s when the use of these steel shipping containers became widespread thanks in part to the United

States military and commercial shipping businesses that actually manufactured similar units in-house.

It was the US Army that developed the idea to put corrugations on the steel walls to increase durability without having to increase the amount of steel needed for the structure. It was also the first type of container to have double end doors and improved on the rolling structure first applied to the Laadkisten unit.

This particular shipping container unit was shared with other countries like Korea for example where it was successfully used for commercial purposes. The US Army's container prototype was later improved upon with the new version having the well-known stacking feature.

As the years progressed, engineers continued their work to improve the design and function of the intermodal shipping container. They were made to last longer and be more reliable in the safe transportation of various products across different channels. When the 1970s arrived, a specific set of standards applicable on a global scale was established for these containers allowing for consistent transporting, loading, and unloading of goods across different ports.

By having one set of standards for everybody, transport became more efficient, saving everyone lots of time and money. These days, intermodal shipping containers continue to be used around the world but they carry an additional purpose and that is to stand as structural blocks for residences and other livable shelters.

Chapter 3:
Understanding the Pros and Cons
of Shipping Container Homes

Before understanding how a shipping container home can benefit you, it is important for you to be mindful of the disadvantages that often come with this type of home. It starts with challenging temperature and humidity control.

DISADVANTAGES

Shipping containers are made entirely out of steel and metals are known to be excellent conductors of heat. If used in areas where daily temperatures are at high levels, the experience will truly be a discomfort. Picture living in a steel oven. When used in areas where temperatures tend to fall quite fast, the container can also become extremely cold in an instant.

Containers call for a little bit more than basic insulation to combat extreme weather conditions. In some cases, multiple layers of insulating materials including brick, wood, and padding may be required if the shipping containers will be utilized for residential purposes.

Because the steel absorbs heat and cold fairly easily, temperature changes can easily cause moisture to over-develop. Given the isolated space, water beads can make the environment clammy. If left unattended to, rust will start to form. The problem with rust is that the minute it starts developing, it will continue to do so, slowly inching its way across the steel frame of the cargo unit.

Design limitations are another con when it comes to these types of homes. Although one of the advantages of shipping containers is that they can be stacked together to allow for a larger living area, the problem with these cargo units is that although they can be stacked, builders are limited to containers of a default dimension. If these containers were to be opened at one side and connected horizontally, it will take additional time, effort, and expense – but it is definitely possible.

Container homes can be constructed on or off site but there is a catch. Given the significant size of the units, they need to be transported using heavy machinery like forklifts and cranes. If the intended space where the home is to reside cannot accommodate the large equipment, there is no way for the container units to be transferred or delivered.

There are also certain building regulations that bind these structures. Building regulations depend on the area, zone, and purpose. There are certain rules which restrict the types of homes that can be built per location. Shipping container homes are not allowed in certain cities or neighborhoods so this can be a problem for the homeowner. Check with your local council, housing authority or government before building a shipping container home.

Securing a permit for construction may be close to if not impossible in some areas. Aside from container units per se, some places do not allow steel buildings to be built so this is another concern that has to be addressed.

Moving onto the internal part of the structure used for shipping container homes, because of the nature of the material used in making shipping container homes, there are certain locational regulations that demand flooring to be treated with specialized insecticides prior to the installation of wooden flooring, tiles, or carpets.

For shipping containers, the floors should be treated with a copper, chromium, and arsenic solution to kill off and prevent bacterial growth over time. If the floor area is not made of steel, any layering should be removed completely and disposed of prior to human habitation.

And unless you are working with a brand-new shipping container, cargo spillage will always be an issue that you have to address early on during your build. Shipping containers are used to transfer various products across borders. In some cases, they carry non-perishable items but there are instances when they are used for perishable food products not to mention cargo that may be of a radioactive or dangerous nature, like chemicals, for example.

Spillage cannot be prevented at all times so contaminants, some of which are undetectable, may leak onto the container. If a homeowner does not ensure proper cleansing prior to the build, this can lead to extreme and costly repercussions later on. Significant expense is necessary to clean a shipping container as abrasive cleansing is needed to be followed by sealant application.

Shipping containers are manufactured to cater to the purpose of storage or the transport of goods across countries. They are not designed to be lived in, so most manufacturers make use of standard materials and solvents in the fabrication process. There are solvents used in painting or sealing the steel that can be harmful to humans even after they dry up. Again, to make a cargo unit suitable for living in, the steel should be stripped raw using abrasive materials and toner sealants.

A used shipping container, before it is used to make a home, may also suffer from expected weathering and structural damage. Even the strongest materials are prone to wear and tear. As cargo shipping containers are used, they bear damage from friction, not to mention collisions from improper handling. There are times when the force of heavy loads adds to the damage as well.

Some of the common damages seen in these units include twisted frames, pin holes, and cracked welds or seals. Although these can be repaired, it will cost a pretty penny to do so. However, if the damages are not addressed in time, rust may form causing even more problems for the builder planning on using them to build a home.

Never forget that these structures have weak areas as well. The thing about steel shipping containers is that they are built to last. Because they are used for imports and exports and are exposed to harsh handling, not to mention weather conditions, they are reinforced on all corners.

Like all structures, these cargo units have their weak spots and one is on the roof. Standard shipping units can only accommodate a limit of about three hundred kilograms at a time. If a homeowner wants a multi-level shipping container home, this imposed but essential limit can easily reduce the potential of converting a space to meet specific living preferences.

Depending on the prospective shipping container homeowner, these cons might be enough to discourage them from making an investment into this housing type - but it is a good thing to know how they can benefit from it and where problems may arise so that they can make an informed decision to move forward or scrap the idea completely.

Now that all of the potential disadvantages of shipping container homes have been laid out, let us move on to the things that make them beneficial for those who are interested in this type of modern-age residential living.

ADVANTAGES

These days, earning a decent living is hard enough. With plenty of restrictions on income for most people, finding cost-effective measures of daily living matters tremendously, and this is one of the main reasons why there are individuals choosing to live in shipping container homes. Compared with other residential options in the market, they offer relatively cheap but desirable accommodation.

Using shipping containers, it is possible to get hundreds of square feet of livable space at a fraction of the price of conventional homes. In the long run, the cost savings exceed rent savings as well. Not bad for owned property. If you are interested in exceptional value for money, this is a home option that you should definitely consider.

Shipping container homes are also some of the most environmentally-friendly buildings available today. From solar panels to energy conserving LED lights, modern times have grown to embrace environmentally friendly products and services.

Shipping container homes are in their own right eco-friendly housing options as there are thousands of these containers that are recycled into homes eliminating the need to manufacture additional building materials to satisfy the residential and commercial development demand. Recycling the steel instead of melting it down or scrapping also reduces the need for energy required for processing.

Building a shipping container home also allows for an efficient construction timetable to be put into play. Because the initial structure already exists, fabricating a residence from shipping containers can be done in a short amount of time as compared with other types of homes.

Having an efficient construction timetable means that homeowners get to enjoy their new house faster and have to incur fewer costs to do so. In construction, every day of work translates to significant expenses in labor. It is possible to prepare, build, wire, insulate, and decorate shipping container homes in a few weeks to a couple of months' time.

Want the structure to be constructed off-site? This is not impossible when it comes to a shipping container home. Shipping container homes can be built on any parcel of land, even an enclosed garage, and can be transported to their final location later on.

This viability for off-site construction is one of the many things that make this residential option extremely appealing. There are instances when certain areas are not conducive for building. It can be because of the limited space or the unavailability of constant sources of energy making the use of heavy duty power tools hassling.

Access is also relatively easy. When you need a shipping container, it is fairly simple to source one for your build. As countries continue to engage in import and export trading, shipping containers will be readily available. Hundreds of thousands of these containers are used, reused, and repurposed, making the concept of container homes easily justifiable not to mention highly sustainable.

Because of their primary purpose to transport products across continents, shipping containers have been built to satisfy transportation standards for shipment. Homeowners can easily have these transported via truck, rail, or ship, whichever works best.

You will also benefit from their structural durability. Shipping containers are very strong, not to mention durable. Apart from being fabricated from steel, these were designed to withstand constant exposure to the elements together with heavy loads and rough handling.

They can stand up to earthquakes and other disasters thanks to their welded modular design. This is why they are excellent materials to use for home construction projects.

These easily comply with ISO standards and have the ability to be stacked in multiple tiers. As they come equipped with built-in interlocking corner supports, fabricating multiple level homes using containers is safe, not to mention easy to do. Those interested in a cost-effective and long-lasting residential solution will find shipping container homes truly beneficial.

Their modular design is another advantage. Shipping containers carry a standard modular design. All containers carry the same width dimensions. In some cases, they differ by height and length but that is about it.

There are two standard measurements for the latter, so sourcing the right sized containers is still as easy as pie. Aside from making residential design planning a breeze, it makes transport as simple as possible too. The modular design can also be attributed to the interlocking quality of these containers.

Its modular design, interlocking components, and built-in support corners reduce the need for additional labor during the home construction process. Homeowners can easily cut costs on steel cutting and welding to name a few. When it comes to the design process, it only takes simple modifications to make the space adequate for living.

Finally, its limited need for any building foundation does not only make builds easy, but fairly cheap as well. There is really no need to spend time on extensive foundational support as basic systems will work just fine.

Shipping containers are designed in such a way that they have four support corners readily able to fit other containers and hold them in place. For as long as significant ground foundation is laid out, the structure will be good to go.

Given these pros and cons of shipping containers, it is up to you to weigh them out and see if a shipping container home is something that will benefit you both in the short and long run.

Chapter 4:
Initial Preparations When Constructing a Shipping Container Home

Just like with any type of construction, you need to prepare the materials that you will be using for the build, and this starts with checking building regulations in your area, securing the necessary permits, and hiring the necessary professionals to help you out.

Building a house from shipping containers does not make it less of a structure and this is why permits and licenses are still necessary. You might encounter contractors or building agents that will suggest forgoing permits to cut costs. Although offers like this are somewhat attractive, it is a trap that you should not fall for. If you do, you will be in violation of local ordinances.

Not only can you be fined for it but you will miss out on vital inspections that will ensure that your structure is up to code, meaning that it is safe to live in. Without the necessary permits during the initial build, homeowners will also have a difficult time selling off the property when the time comes to do so.

The process of securing permits together with local building code compliance are two of the most challenging hurdles that come with building shipping container houses. Because of its relatively new concept, and also due to the highly specialized niche market, there is currently no clear cut system in place.

Standard building practices are applied when this type of infrastructure is constructed. Before an occupancy permit is granted by local housing agency officials, the homeowner must meet basic health and safety standards for the project. Building plans should be presented for approval and a final inspection is to be conducted after the build is completed.

When it comes to the building plans, it is possible for homeowners to draft these themselves, as long as they meet the requirements of the local housing agency. In some cases, the absence of an architect's stamp may fly but only for the initial draft. All plans for final approval must have the support and final outlay of a licensed architect, lest they be rejected.

The stamp ensures that a licensed professional has seen the plans and is taking responsibility for the integrity and design of the structure about to be built. If something were to happen, accidents for example, as a result of these plans, all liabilities will befall the architect. Shipping containers used for storage purposes no longer need this stamp but those to be used as homes do.

The need for permits may also stem from area classification. In most cases, permits are no longer needed in areas belonging to farm, ranch, or agricultural zones. Zoning is a matter that you need to pay attention to.

Each zone has a distinct set of building and occupancy regulations that should be followed to a T. Making the mistake of missing out on satisfying even a single rule can lead to the building being deemed unfit for use. Aside from hefty fines and penalties, the structure could be torn down.

A good thing about zones is that they are pretty easy to check. Simply pay the local building department a visit and have your zone verified right then and there. Aside from checking zones and the regulations that they come with, you can also ask the same agency whether or not shipping container homes can be built in the area.

They can also provide information on the specific permits needed for the construction if the zone allows for such infrastructures to stand. Be sure to note down who provided the information so that you have a name to mention should there be problems with regulations later on.

Especially if you will be obtaining the services of a general contractor, he or she can process all permits and licenses on your behalf. You do have the option of obtaining your own building permits as well but this will take time.

You can even choose to build the structure yourself but only do so if you possess the same level of skills as the local contractors, builders, draftsmen, and architects in your area. If not, it would be logical not to mention cost-effective to let the professionals handle this task.

With shipping containers, the ones used to make homes are usually pre-owned. Unless they are sourced brand new, the homeowner must also obtain the necessary clearance from the health department deeming the container clean and safe enough to be converted into residential space.

In some cases, these containers are used to ship perishable products commonly resulting in the development of bacterial residue. Used to transport other products, these can be left in cargo holding stations for months to years at a time leading to rust formation and the like. All of the shells have to be cleaned out via sand and water blasting and sealed for preservation before being used to construct a home.

Depending on your skill level and knowledge when it comes to construction, apart from regular builders, you might also want to get the help of a licensed contractor. It is always a wise decision to consult a reliable home contractor when

Sourcing through referrals is usually the best option here as people have had a first-hand experience as to the kind of work a contractor can provide. They have seen them at work and can provide a certain level of expectation. Start by consulting family, friends, and neighbors that have had construction work done recently.

Keep in mind that even if a contractor was referred to you, it is still necessary for you to run a complete background check and interview. It is a good idea to consider three to five potential applicants for your construction needs.

Doing so provides you with options, especially since these professionals may come to offer varying skills and services. The most challenging aspect of any build, for a homeowner, is not the work itself but locating a competent contractor who can deliver quality output in a timely manner.

When conducting your background check, work with local agencies, preferably those handling consumer affairs, or a chapter of the Better Business Bureau operating in your area. Check for blacklists, complaint histories, and the like. One or two offenses may be acceptable, within reason of course, but take repeated offenses as a red flag.

Aside from checking a contractor's work history, check for licensing records as well. A contractor must pass a standard competency examination to be issued a license. The absence of this legal document also signals a red flag, possibly an illegal or limited practice.

Keep in mind though that possessing a license does not equate with excellent workmanship. This is still something left for the client to decide. A license offers the sense of professionalism and commitment to the job at hand.

Insurance is essential. A contractor should be insured and the homeowner should have ample insurance coverage as well. Coverage for physical injuries on site, property damage, and natural disasters are necessary. See to it that a working comprehensive policy is in order before any of the work begins.

Oftentimes, a construction project requires several contractors --- a general contractor and subcontractors working under his or her command. The number of contractors needed for a build depends on the size of the project and the requirements imposed upon by the homeowner.

A general contractor works by organizing the work schedule, securing the necessary permits, and coordinating with materials suppliers. The subcontractors serve to handle specific elements of the build. One may be hired to handle all of the electrical work and utilities while another may be in charge of built-in furnishings or external landscaping.

In some cases, general contractors have teams of subcontractors that they can refer. If this network is unavailable, it will be the homeowner's responsibility to find these specialists one by one.

Searching for contractors is only one part of the equation. What follows is getting a bid from each prospect being considered. A written bid is necessary as it can be transformed into a binding contract. With any type of construction project, every correspondence has to be on paper.

Be sure to get bids covering the same job tasks or output, manpower requirements, materials sourcing, and the like. This will make it easier for you to choose the best contractor to hire. Engaging in price negotiations during the bidding process is fine as long as all requests from both parties are reasonable. All bids and negotiations should be finalized before any contract is signed, as altering parts of it later on can lead to more expenses on your part.

Just like any other product or service in the market, being cheap does not make it the best considerable option. In this line of work, price usually dictates quality. A home is something that is meant to last for a long time so paying a bit more for better output is worth doing.

By paying more, a homeowner will not only be entitled to a better effort from the builders but better materials as well. Even if the costs are higher in the short run, the generated savings in the long run will be greater.

In negotiating a fair contract, make sure that the document spells out all the terms of the work involved as this will help both parties reduce or eliminate the occurrence of time-consuming and costly misunderstandings during the build. Here are the initial pieces of information that the contract should carry.

- Contractor's Name and Contact Information

- Contractor's License Information

- Subcontractors' Names and Contact Information

- Homeowners Name and Contact Information

- Agreed Upon Work Timetable including Start and Finish Dates

- Agreed Upon Mode of Payment and Payment Schedule

- Scope of Work that might include Securing Permits

- List of Specific Materials Needed

- List of Machinery and Equipment Needed

- Demolition and Clean-Up Provisions

- Terms of the Agreement

- Arbitration Provisions or Dispute Clauses

- Limitations of Liability for the Homeowner or Code Violations and Contractor Obligation

- Insurance Provisions

- Signatures of Both Parties and the Date of Signing

- Addendum for Non-Inclusions to the Contract

Construction projects are normally done in phases and payments follow suit as they are settled in stages over the course of the build. This includes the delivery of key supplies and materials. A contractor will require a down payment of about ten percent or so.

Protect yourself by not paying more than what is necessary during this stage. In most cases, even with initially trustworthy contractors, they have the tendency of using excess payments to finance projects of other clients, oftentimes leaving the financier, you, high and dry as time passes.

Always be in communication with contractors. Aside from receiving frequent project updates, this enables all parties to resolve problems as early as possible. Resolving issues during the course of the build is better than having to attend to them after the turnover.

Contractors, during the build, are keener on fixing problems like leaking roofs or faulty wiring and the like. Getting them to attend to these issues later on will be quite the challenge as they have already received payment for the initial service and won't be at a loss for the sloppy output.

A good security measure to ensure that you are extended reasonable aftercare services is to include a clause in the contract allowing you to hold the final payment installment for a month after the turnover.

Aside from ensuring that all construction as per your specifications are met a hundred percent, the full payment to the main contractor should only be given after you have obtained signed documents covering payments to subcontractors, suppliers, and other expenses for the build.

These official release papers are called mechanic's-lien waivers. They stand as receipts for services and products received. Without the formal release from obligation, these agencies can have a mechanic's lien placed against your house until all payables have been settled. Demand these waivers together with official receipts for all purchases and expenses from the general contractor.

Do not hesitate to ask. Here is an initial series of questions that you can ask the person who made the referral.

- Were you satisfied with the output?

- Was construction completed on time?

- Would you rehire this contractor?

- Were there issues with daily cleanup?

- Was the contractor approachable?

- Was the contractor open to sudden plan alterations?

- Did the contractor have his own team of workers?

- Did the contractor have his own materials suppliers?

- What was the agreed upon mode of payment and schedule?

Significant effort is necessary but there are ways by which homeowners can spot questionable contractors. Here are red flags that you should be mindful of.

- Special or Bargain Prices

- High-Pressure Tactics or Overselling

- Refusal to Quote a Total Cost for the Build

- Failure to Provide Work References

- Unverifiable License Information

- Unverifiable Insurance Details

- Unverifiable Contact Information

- Non-existent Affiliation to Recognized Industry Associations

- Unsolicited Contact

- Leftover Material Accumulation

Chapter 5:
Working on the Actual Build

Shipping containers can be bought new and if so, they no longer need to be prepped before the build. If a homeowner has decided on purchasing being transformed into any living space, may it be an office or an actual house. Part of the health and safety standards require that the units be stripped raw and cleaned out prior to reuse.

When used for cargo, these containers may have been used to transport items that leak harmful chemicals and bacteria over time. Given enough time to culture, these can produce harmful vapors that oftentimes have no visible marks or scent - making them dangerously undetectable.

It is important that any dirt, dust, or debris are removed from the container. Abrasive materials, bristled brooms, and the like may be used for this process. If a pressure washer is available, then use it to greatly expedite the cleaning process. It would be best to get the help of a professional when it comes to any pressure washing as the process can overwhelm a non-expert.

Start at the end of the container moving your way towards the main doors. Pay a lot of attention to the seams, the nooks, and all crannies you see. Check the floors for wear and tear as well. Excessive damage can raise a red flag.

Start cleaning the inside then move your way out of the container. If a pressure washer is used, it may be powerful enough to strip off any old paint not to mention rust that has formed on the steel. Any excess corrosion that cannot be initially removed can be treated with acidic compounds like vinegar.

To hasten the process, rub the vinegar in using pieces of aluminum foil. Depending on the gravity of the rust situation, industrial cleaners may also be used. If the corrosion is excessive and has caused other, more serious, damages to the unit, it may be best to simply forego the particular container.

After it dries, do a secondary cleaning run by going over the container with some medium grit sandpaper on a belt or orbital sander. This serves the purpose of removing any remaining paint flakes. You do not have to strip off all of the old paint, just the areas which show signs of wear because if you don't, the new paint that you apply will peel off in no time.

Prime the container to seal it against corrosion and any moisture. You can then apply any paint color of your choosing to the interior and exterior walls of the shipping container.

If the builder needs to cut portions out of any side walls, the cutting and sanding should be done prior to the priming and painting. This will save the builder a lot of time and money. When choosing paints, thicker solutions work best for steel shipping containers. Not only do they offer stronger and longer-lasting external seals, but thick paints also stick better to the metal structures.

Building any type of house, regardless of the size, is never a small feat. Aside from multiple materials and machinery, a number of tasks must also be accomplished by competent builders and design professionals. Part of the appeal of shipping container homes is the simplification of the construction process that it offers.

Before general construction begins, obtain all necessary permits and source materials from reliable suppliers. Also form a team of laborers depending on the magnitude of the task at hand. If a contractor is hired, he or she will be the one to handle these.

General construction begins with site work. This involves finding a designated location for the shipping container home. This is the time for groundwork. It may necessitate some excavation to lay the foundation in. At this time, plans for utilities, water management, and septic systems must also be laid out.

The size of the main ground foundation depends on how many containers are included in the design plans and how much weight is expected to be held after construction is completed. The foundation should be strong enough to keep everything in place even when disasters like typhoons or earthquakes hit.

The foundation can be built using precast concrete panels to make things easier for the builder. If a homeowner can afford the time, a stronger foundation can be created using hollow cement blocks and poured concrete.

This goes atop an excavated area that can be filled with gravel to assist with drainage. As the foundation is laid out, builders can add insulating elements and water proofing components for a better final structure.

The process of setting the building's foundation is the trickiest step in the project because it must also address gas supply lines, utilities, and electrical wiring components. These are run from the base of the foundation to their respective positions in the home's floor plan.

After all of these are taken care of, there is a matter of sealing the main foundation. Traditional methods make use of compacted soil, gravel, laid-out rebar, and more concrete on-pour.

Shipping containers have been designed to carry a modular outlay but these bodies can be modified to fit the needs of the homeowner. Although the corrugated steel walls have been fabricated to support heavy loads not to mention constant exposure to the elements, these can be cut to specifications with the proper equipment.

In cases where modular units are placed side by side, not simply stacked atop one another, openings for internal entryways and windows can be cut into the units.

When it comes to these types of modifications, simple as they may seem, it would be best for professionals to be called in for assistance. Aside from an expert builder, a structural engineer, and an architect should also be contacted.

This is because removing a portion of any wall or corner can significantly weaken the structure, reducing the weight that its roof can support. Aside from steel-cutting; welding and framing are other elements involved in the general construction of shipping container homes.

Although these are important parts of the project, they can come at an expense and this is why modifications should only be done when extremely necessary.

After the foundation sets and the container units are prepared for final assembly, it is time to secure them to the foundation and each other. Each base unit is to be crane-lifted onto the foundation, hooked, and welded down. Because of the weight of these container units, it does not take much to secure them into place.

Corner fasteners are all that is necessary to hold them onto the foundation. Additional support can be installed through the use of corner concrete blocks. Containers can then be secured to one another, vertically or horizontally, by making welds. If several units are to be stacked atop one another, additional support beams as dictated by the structural engineer should be utilized.

Internal and external entryways, windows, and other openings should then be framed. The most common method used by builders for shipping container homes begins with steel frames which are then reinforced by wooden ones.

Because of the limited amount of living space provided by cargo units, sliding doors and windows are commonly used. In this case, the steel and wood double frames can be made to run on wheels through L-section panels.

The house is now ready for insulation to be installed. Utility systems and electrical wiring are also run through the home at this point. When the walls have been sealed and all finishes completed, interior plans from painting to furniture arrangements to the installation of fixtures are then satisfied.

Depending on the location, external landscaping may be necessary to add to the home's aesthetic value. Everything then goes under inspection before a certificate of occupancy can be attained.

Given the often miniscule size of shipping container homes, as compared to its traditional residential structural counterparts, this process will take several weeks to several months to complete. The steps are fairly similar to constructing a traditional house, but are faster to complete.

Homeowners that have adequate skills in building can tackle a project like this themselves, but for most, the best route is to go with professional laborers.

A very important part of the construction process for shipping container homes is insulation. Given the type of structure builders will be working with, it is necessary for above standard insulation methods to be applied. The need for insulation depends on where the container home will be placed. Locations where temperatures can rise or fall with ease demand insulation.

Insulation is an important component to any house build. It can come at quite at expense but will save the homeowner from intense temperatures not to mention prevent or reduce the home's susceptibility to condensation which is responsible for rust and mold formation.

Given that the home requires insulation, the next question to ask pertains to how much insulation is necessary and what type of material will work best to satisfy this measure. Colder climates call for more insulation to keep a shipping container home warm. Insulation in this case serves the secondary purpose of controlling condensation.

Usually, cold environments are prone to excessive rainfall. When deciding over insulating materials, this is another aspect that has to be considered. Aside from keeping the steel structure warm, creating a seamless barrier against rain is also necessary.

In areas with a warmer climate, insulation may be necessary but not in the same amount. Here, insulation is needed to prevent as much heat as possible from being absorbed by the steel structure. The goal now is to keep the internal temperature of the home at a relatively low and comfortable, livable level.

Chapter 6:
How Much Will It Cost?

With the housing market in a vulnerable stage and with a majority of people having difficulties affording rent, there is always the continuous hunt for cheaper, more affordable forms of housing. The concept of tiny house living has grown tremendously popular through recent years and it has given rise to alternative forms of housing, including shipping container homes.

But shipping container houses have grown larger in the past years with some measuring as large as traditional homes without as much of a cost. Shipping container homes, or the steel cargo units used in making them, primarily originate from China and other parts of Asia. They are actually considered to be some of the most popular exports received by countries across the globe.

These cargo units allow for the safe and secure delivery of different products across oceans and also serve the purpose of standing as building blocks for unique and environmentally friendly homes. These days, a huge number of international freight are delivered in steel containers that can be stacked upon each other and stored on ship decks, offloaded onto tractor trailer backs, and carted into trains.

In some cases, these cargo containers are shipped back to the source for reuse. Other times, they are stored empty in shipment container graveyards. There are ways to recycle these containers if they are no longer meant to be reused. It is possible to scrap the steel or melt it down or the containers can be cleaned out and used as building blocks for shipping container homes.

The latter promotes the lowest carbon footprint making it a viable solution to the need and demand for ample housing around the world. Thanks to the influence of architects, these units have not only been converted into storage houses but residential homes, guest houses, studios, offices, retail store spaces, and many more.

Container units come prefabricated with a couple of standard sizes. To make them suitable for residential living, architects have found a way to modify them increasing the amount of livable space that homeowners interested in shipping container homes can enjoy.

When positioned side by side, these can provide thousands of square footage which can further be increased by having containers stacked atop one another. The cost of this kind of home depends primarily on how many shipping containers will be used during construction.

It starts with the type of shipping container to be used. These can be bought new or used. New ones definitely cost more while used container units can be bought for several hundred dollars to three thousand dollars on average. What homeowners get for this amount is a complete structure readily available for modification.

Made out of solid steel and welded together in the best possible way, these structures are extremely durable and offer an excellent, yet cost-effective base or foundation for a house meant to be lived in for years on end.

The only catch with shipping container homes is that more often than not it is the homeowner who must own the land that it resides in. Aside from purchasing the container units and spending on the land, homeowners must also shoulder various costs which include the securing of permits, utilities connections, electricity grid connections, and gas connections to name a few.

Depending on the homeowner, he or she can reduce the carbon footprint even more by installing solar panels in the home. A basic solar setup would cost about five thousand dollars depending on how green a homeowner wants to go. There are people who live completely off the grid and have a complex solar panel setup in their shipping container home.

Although it may come at a large initial expense, it generates an excess of savings over time. With this type of home, it can be built in a relatively short period of time. This means that labor expenses usually measure to about a third of what a traditional house may cost to build or renovate.

For those who want to live in a shipping container home, provided that they have the land to house it in and their area permits this type of residence, here are the initial sources of expense that come with such a project.

- Steel Containers
- Site preparation (foundation)
- Assembly and modification of cargo units
- Installation of insulation, heating, and cooling systems
- Plumbing
- Electricity
- Roofing
- Flooring
- Furnishings

- Windows and entryways

- External landscaping

- Other finishing

The thing about shipping container homes is that they can be built off-site and delivered to the final location ready to be lived in. If this is the option chosen by the homeowner, he or she should add the corresponding shipping costs to the total expense. Depending on how far the delivery point is, this can amount to several thousand dollars of additional expense.

An amount as little as $20,000 can provide an ample shelter complete with a front porch. This amount can easily yield a 350 square foot home that is perfect for a bachelor's pad. For this type of home, construction will usually take several weeks to a couple of months.

Before investing in this type of house, it is good to plan everything from assuring the availability of land, securing permits, checking local zoning and building regulations, and setting aside a reasonable budget for the build. Usually, overall costs go beyond what was originally quoted.

So as not to be overwhelmed by any additional expense, it would be wise to set aside an additional ten to twenty percent of the total budget for emergency needs.

Chapter 7:
Some Design Ideas to Consider

When it comes to a shipping container home, if homeowners will be sticking to a standard structure with minimal modifications and a limited amount of space, then they should plan their home design accordingly. There are plenty of excellent sources for space-saving floor plans that will allow homeowners to have several fully-functional areas in a modular unit.

Depending on the available square footage, homeowners should focus on four main areas. These are the bedroom, bathroom, kitchen, and living areas. Generally, the living area should have the largest space allotment out of the four as it will be the place where the most amount of time will be spent.

It would be best to combine the kitchen and living area into a free flowing space which will also serve the purpose of acting as a convertible dining area.

The bedroom can exist with or without a separate wall or door. If without, it is a great idea to use simple wall dividers that can provide the necessary privacy without taking up too much room in the modular unit.

Wall dividers can easily be positioned to increase or decrease the amount of available space in each area. If there is a room that needs the utmost privacy, it will be the bathroom. It would be best to secure this with a lockable door, but go with sliding ones instead of traditional swivels due to space limitations in a container.

When planning a shipping container home, everything should be decided according to the specific needs of the homeowner. A good move would be to work closely with an architect and an interior designer who can provide the best insight as to how a space can be arranged to deliver an outcome that will be up to par.

When it comes to floor plans and design blueprints, homeowners will require the assistance of competent professionals. An architect, a structural engineer, and an interior designer can help determine the best placements for furnishings and divisions for rooms not to mention identify where extra supports may be necessary. Landscapers can provide assistance on the outside part of the home.

The Internet is an excellent place to start looking for ideas prior to the build. There are tons of free resources that can be accessed with the click of a button. Some, more professional, layouts may be obtained for a minimal fee. There are also some sample plans included later in this book!

The beauty of the Internet is that aside from offering a wide variety of options to interested homeowners, it is also a great resource where people can find feedback on these designs; how they work, what can be changed, what is advisable versus what is not, and so on and so forth.

Together with the assistance of professionals, it is extremely important for homeowners to at least have some idea of what they want their home to look like and carry. It will surely make the design process easier and faster for everyone and it will allow for the least amount of expense. With everything identified beforehand, costly mistakes can be avoided.

Depending on how many shipping containers homeowners plan to utilize in their construction, the amount of livable space may be quite limited in certain cases. Because of how shipping container homes are unlike traditional houses in different ways, it is important for potential homeowners to be fully aware of the restrictions that may come with this choice of residence. Not only will there be a more limited amount of space to work with but when container units are stacked, there is also a weight limit for the upper tiers.

To live comfortably despite the lesser or fixed space allotment, homeowners should be mindful not only of their choice of furniture but everything that they bring into the home. If multiple shipping container units will be stacked atop one another, the assistance of a structural engineer should be attained.

The structural engineer will be the one to assess the allowable weight limit for the tiers. In some cases, additional support beams or posts may be installed in the bottom tier to make the upper units as functional and safe as possible.

Since shipping container units come in fixed dimensions, a great way to have access to more space, for as long as the homeowner's budget permits, is to put several containers side by side. With the help of a professional contractor, entryways can be cut into the units and reinforced.

With proper planning, the space restrictions of shipping container homes can easily be counteracted, offering homeowners the possibility of a non-traditional, cost-effective, and highly efficient abode that will last for decades.

For the interior arrangements, here are some ideas that you might want to consider. In the bedroom, the essential pieces of furniture include the bed, a closet, and a bedside table. These days, there are plenty of available sources for multi-functional furniture.

This can mean having storage underneath the bedframe, a nightstand that can function as transformable seating, and a closet that can have a built-in dresser.

The living area will surely be the busiest part of the house. It will also be the primary area where homeowners will be entertaining visitors and guests over time. This is the reason why, even with a limited amount of space, ample seating may be required. It is a good thing that there are plenty of furniture offerings these days that allow for multiple functionalities.

Most home kitchens come equipped with a stove top, an oven, an overhead exhaust, a microwave, a toaster, and a coffee maker. These are the basic appliances that go into a typical kitchen. If the allotted space and budget allows for all of these to be purchased, then by all means purchase them.

If the homeowner wants to keep the space simple but still have that food prep function then the toaster, coffee maker, and microwave may be scrapped from the list. It is fairly easy to heat meals, boil water for coffee, and toast bread on the stove top.

Now comes the bathroom. The rule of thumb for bathrooms is that they should be kept as simple as possible but still be able to satisfy all of the homeowners needs. There are only four components necessary to make a bathroom complete. Here they are: Sink, Toilet, Shower Area, and Storage for Towels and Toiletries.

Chapter 8:
FAQs

1. *Aren't shipping containers sensitive to external conditions? It can get extremely hot or cold inside depending on the weather.*

Shipping containers, when used to make a home, are insulated just like the walls in any traditional house. This will help with temperature and humidity control.

2. *How come shipping containers are difficult to purchase?*

There is a misconception that shipping containers are surplus products. Companies actually reserve them for when they need to have something shipped. Containers that are sold commercially are those which have some age to them. Currently, there is no other way to source these for re-purposing.

3. *Can a shipping container be used right off the bat?*

Shipping containers sold to the public have gone through tons of travel and contained various items, some of which may be in liquid form. Surely, tons of debris have been collected during this time. Pre-treating and thoroughly cleaning these containers, both inside and out, is highly necessary.

4. *Are shipping container homes rust proof?*

These containers are made from durable Corten steel which is coated with ceramic paint. This makes them resilient against rust and corrosion.

5. *Why should I live in a home that looks like it came from the shipping yard?*

Just like other building materials, the container will serve as the foundation for your home. You can then decorate it anyway you like, both internally and externally. Depending on your preference, you can choose to cover it in other materials like wood or stucco that will make it unrecognizable as a shipping container.

6. *Do all neighborhoods allow these types of homes?*

There are building codes and zoning regulations that communities follow. Be sure to check with local authorities on whether or not this type of home is permitted in your area.

Chapter 9:
Sample Floor Plans

The following are some sample floor plans.

Feel free to use any of the following designs to create your own container home, or simply use them to get some ideas!

You can simply combine aspects of the following floor plans you like and their different designs into your own container home as you wish.

The next chapter after this will show you what the finished product looks like, and will give you some cool ideas for the exterior design.

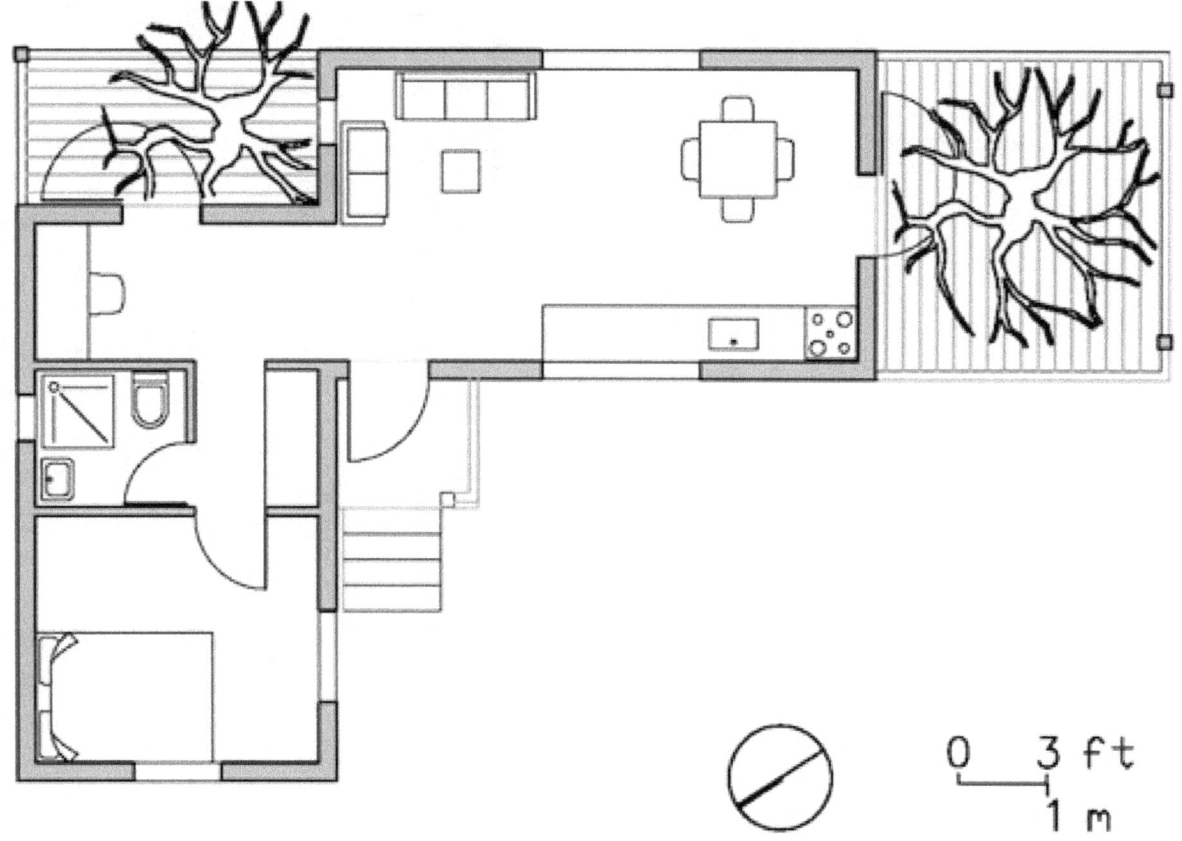

0 3 ft
1 m

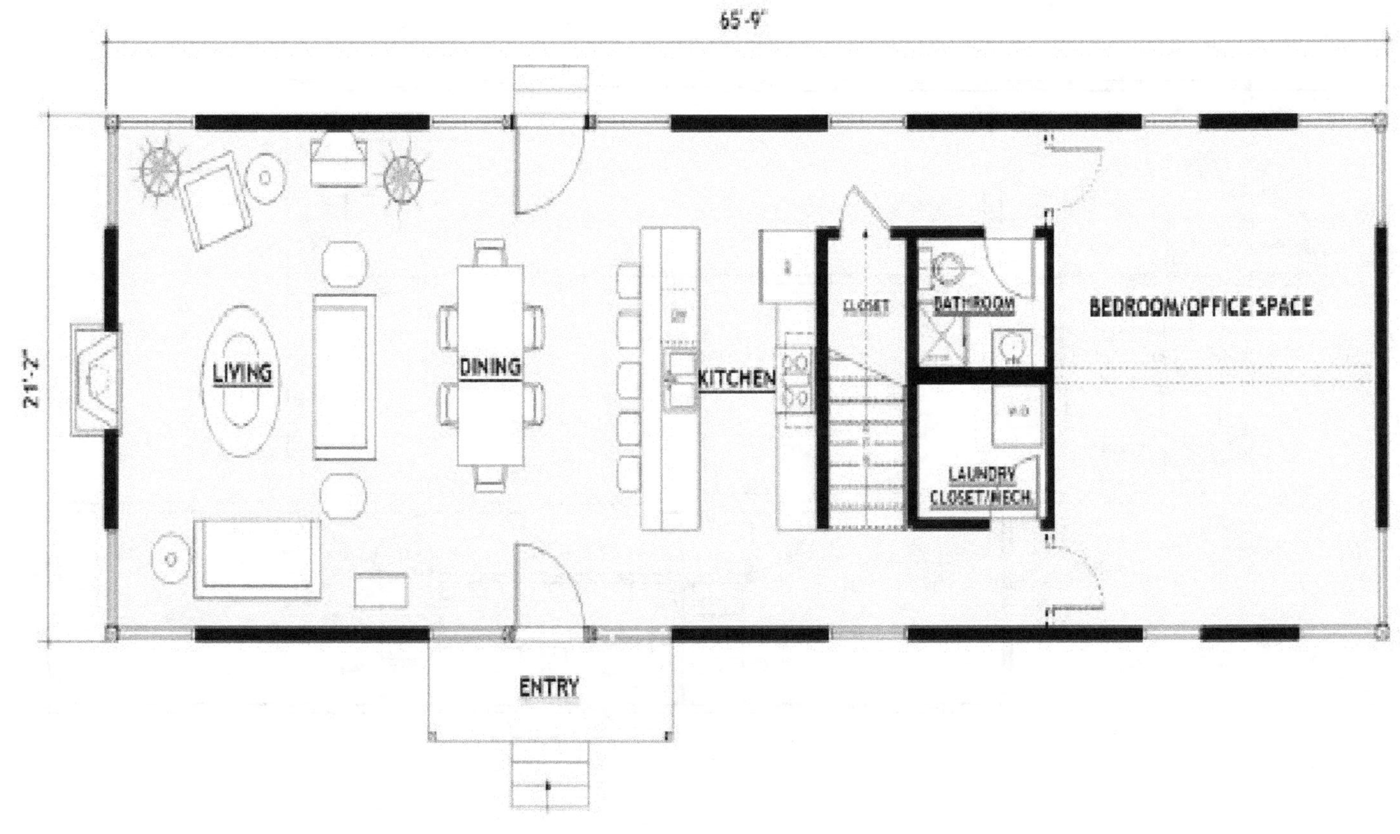

65'-9"
21'-2"
LIVING
DINING
KITCHEN
CLOSET
BATHROOM
BEDROOM/OFFICE SPACE
LAUNDRY CLOSET/MECH.
ENTRY
47

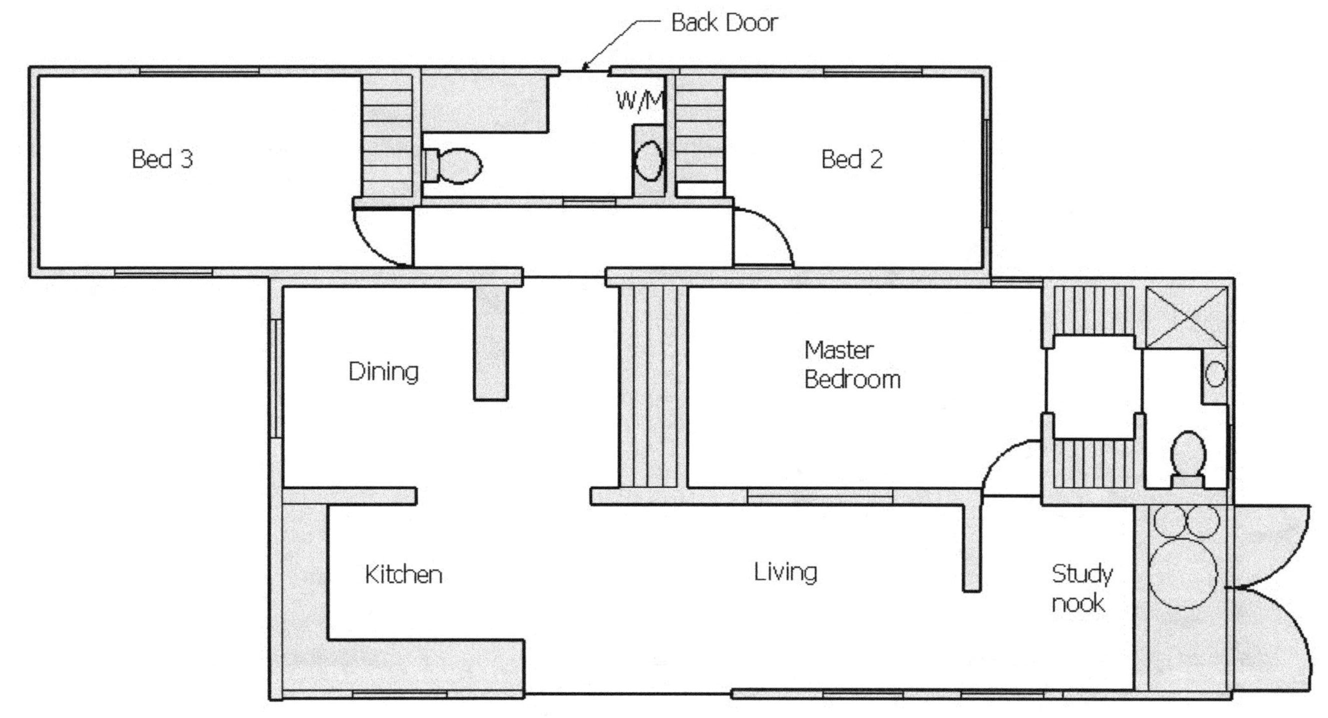

Back Door
Bed 3
W/M
Bed 2
Dining
Master Bedroom
Kitchen
Living
Study nook

HOT WATER
20' - STACKER
COMPOSTING TOILET
STO
SINK
BATH
LINEN
QUEEN BED PEDESTAL STO.
STEP UP
DECK
CLOSET
1 METER STAIRCASE
ENTRY
CORNER MEDIA CTR.
DAYBED SEATING
PULL OUT TABLE
SINK
RANGE
DRYER
WASHER
BATH
REF
PANTRY
1 METER STAIRCASE

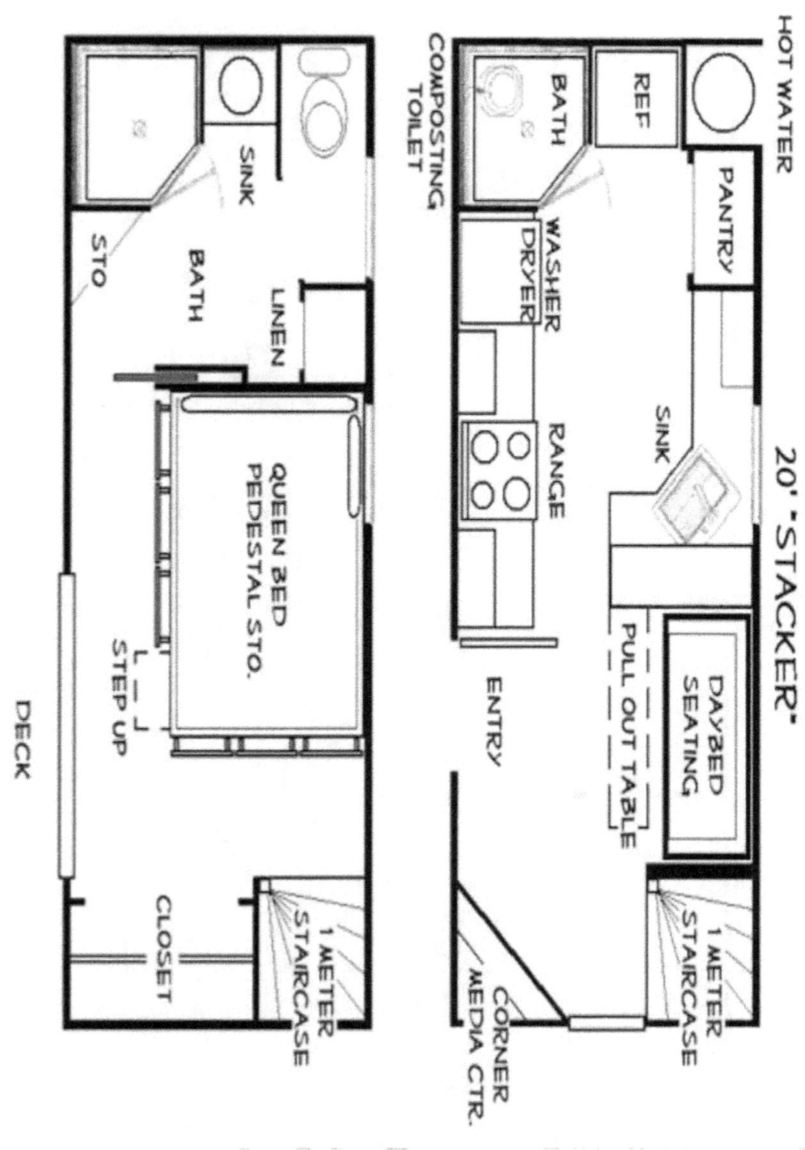

49

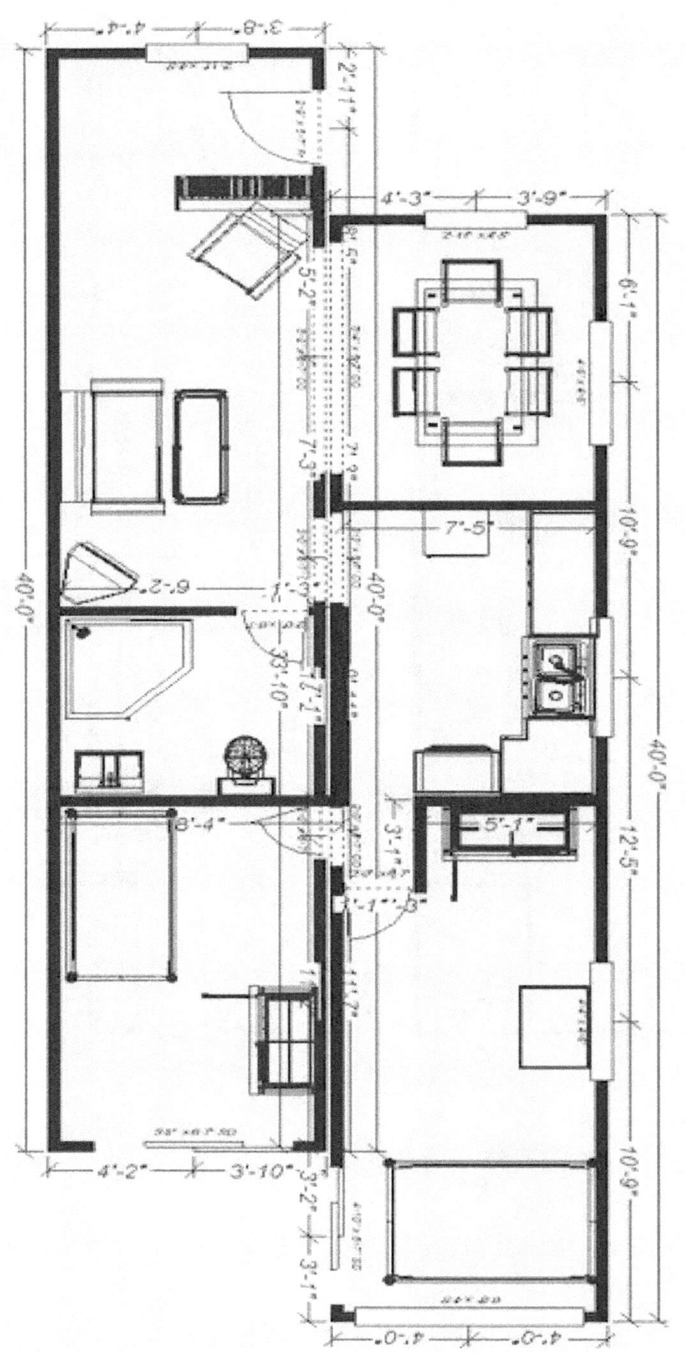

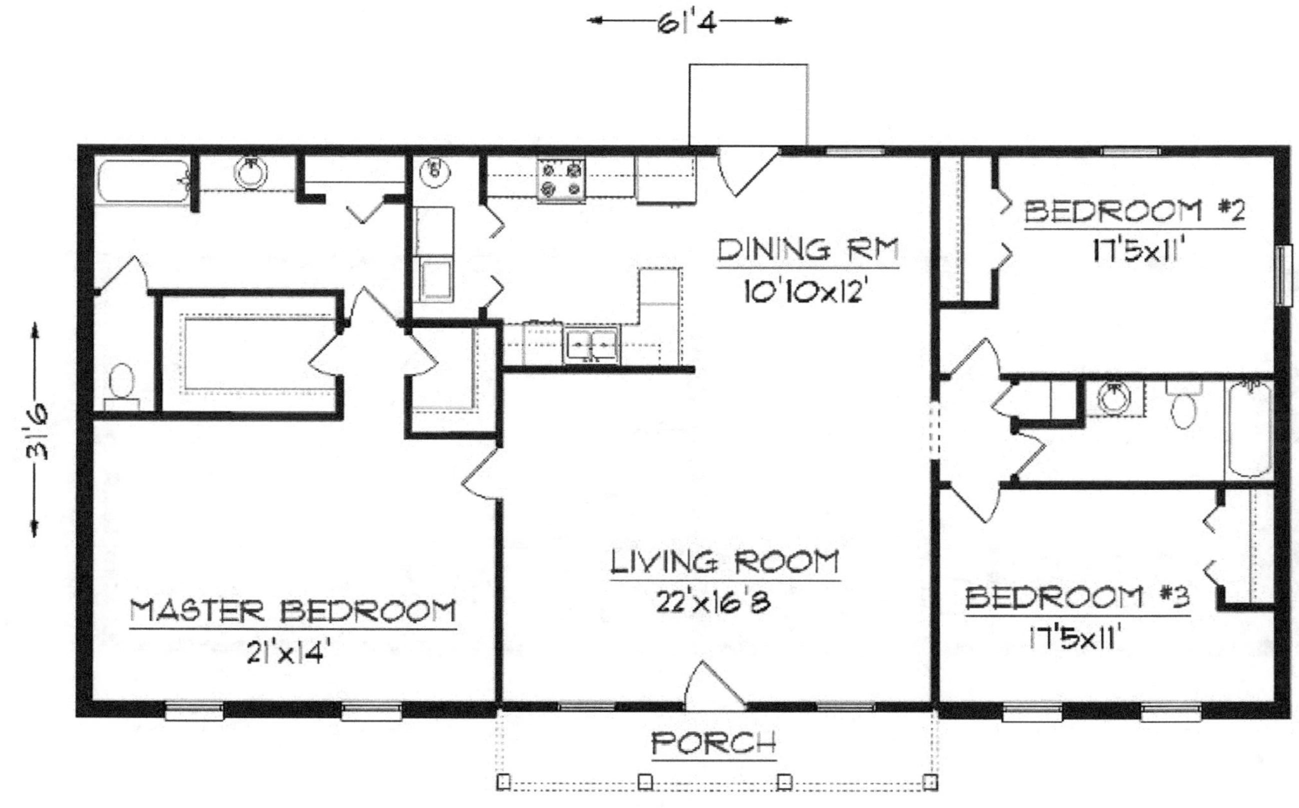
61'4
31'6
DINING RM
10'10x12'
BEDROOM #2
17'5x11'
MASTER BEDROOM
21'x14'
LIVING ROOM
22'x16'8
BEDROOM #3
17'5x11'
PORCH
51

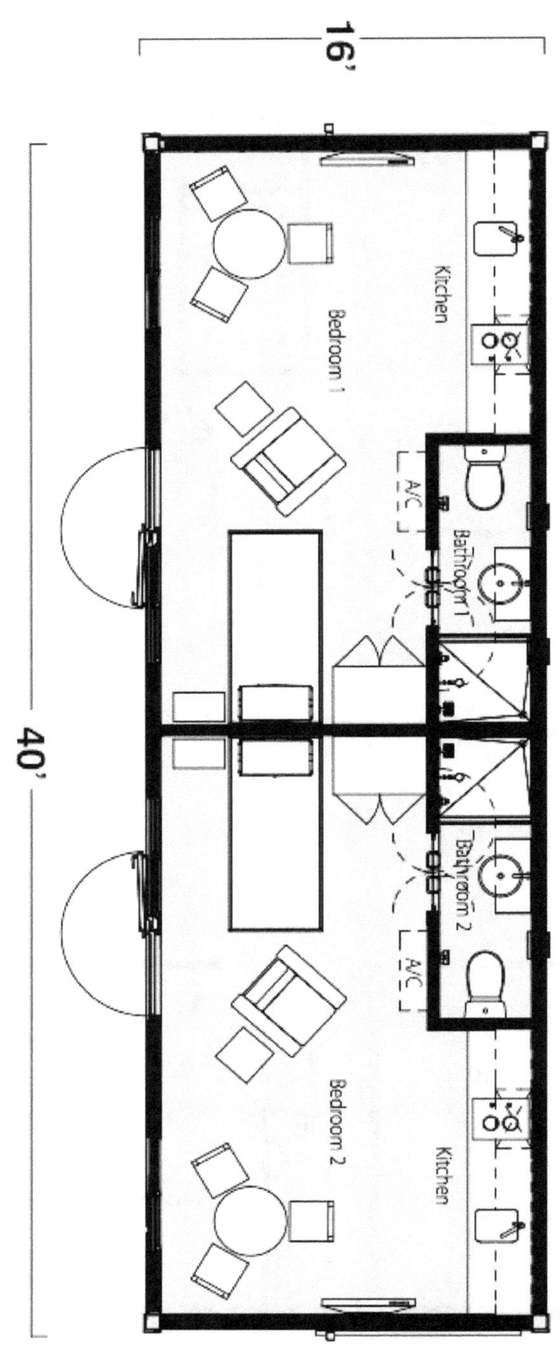

16'
40'
Kitchen
Bedroom 1
A/C
Bathroom 1
Bathroom 2
A/C
Bedroom 2
Kitchen

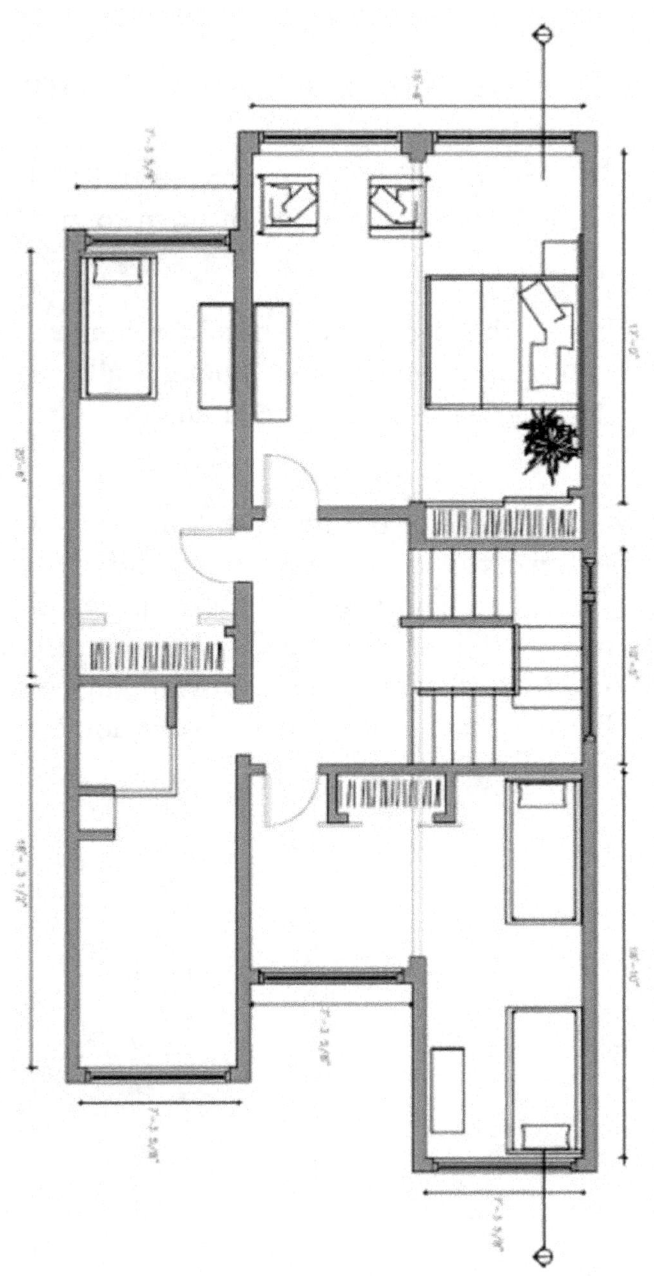

Chapter 10:
The Finished Container Home

This chapter contains a few images of the finished container homes and different design aspects of them to give you some ideas!

As you will see, the designs of container homes vary from extremely simplistic 1-container homes, all the way to elaborate designs with stacked containers and swimming pools.

Also take note of some of the finishes. Some have opted for a timber panel finish to their homes, whilst others leave the bare container showing. A common design is to have a feature wall where the bare container is exposed, while the rest is covered in timber or an alternative exterior. This might be something you would like to consider when having your home designed.

Chapter 11:
How Long Will My Shipping Container Home Last?

An often overlooked question is – 'How long will my shipping container home actually last for?'

Because of the nature of a shipping container home, this is a very logical thing to ask. While the cost of a container home is obviously going to be lower than that of a traditional home, the longevity of such a home needs to come into consideration.

Used Containers VS. New Containers

Whether you built your home with new shipping containers, or with used ones will play a large role in how long your container home actually lasts for before needing repairs.

Your typical used shipping container is an average of 10 years old by the time you purchase it. Keep in mind, this is an average. In some parts of the world you will find used containers for sale that are only 1-2 years old. Make sure you ask the question of how old the container is when making your purchase!

The average container will last 20-25 years before needing any repairs, or being affected too heavily by the weather. So, by purchasing a new container you will get your full 20-25 years of use before any repairs need to be made, whereas with a 2nd hand container you will be looking at only 10-15 years.

Preventative Measures

The preventative measures you implement will play a role in how long your container home stays in good condition.

Doing things like insulating your container, sealing any cracks, making sure your container is re-painted every few years, and rust-proofing your container periodically will play a huge role in the longevity of your containers.

If you take proper care of your home and are diligent in it's up-keep, it is quite possible that major repairs or replacements of the container will never be needed!

External Cladding

Having external cladding on your home can greatly increase its longevity! Rather than having the bare container face the outside world, you may want to consider wooden panels, plaster, brick, render, or some other form of external cladding to protect against the elements.

Weather

The weather where you live will play a huge role in the condition of your container home, and also the amount of up-keep required.

If you live in an extremely hot environment, you will need to use a heavy duty paint, and re-paint your container home often to keep it protected from the sun.

In a cold environment, having proper insulation is vital. Also ensuring that all cracks and holes are sealed is very important as to avoid any leakages and rust within your home. Once again, painting your home and making it rust-proof are very important.

In climates with a wide variance of temperatures you will need to be most careful. Ensuring proper insulation, rust-proofing, sealing of the home, and constant up-keep and inspection is very important.

So... How Long Will It Last?!

There is no exact answer to this question.

Just like any normal home, your container home will require up-keep and repairs over time.

However, with proper care it can potentially stay in good condition for as long as any traditional home.

Chapter 12:
How to Build a Container Home
on the Cheap

Besides from their designs being unique and attractive, and their low environmental impact, most people choose to build a container home because of their low cost.

Chances are that the reason you picked up this book is because you want to make a shipping container home on the cheap.

As discussed, shipping container homes are typically cheaper than your traditional home. But if you aren't careful – the costs can definitely still add up!

When building your container home on a budget, there are a few things you need to consider!

Use Used Containers

This one is obvious, but worth mentioning. You can often find used shipping containers at an extremely small fraction of the price of new ones. Often, the quality is quite comparable also.

But, make sure you inspect your containers thoroughly before purchasing to look for any signs of damage or rust!

Plan Diligently

Plan, plan, plan! Most people spend much more than anticipated on their build because they fail to plan enough.

Constantly changing your mind about what you want can quickly add up. Additional containers and materials can be expensive, and also hiring contractors, architects, and engineers is a large expense.

Think carefully before starting your build, consult with an engineer or architect, finalize your plan, and then stick to it!

Don't Cut Away Too Much Steel

Making a lot of cut-outs in your container will quickly add up!

If you want to save money, then keep your designs simple. Cutting out steel to add multiple windows, doors, and hallways will add rapidly to your cost. Each time you make a cut, you need to pay for some material to fill that space, along with sealing the container.

It sounds simple, but this can really add to your overall cost.

Salvage Local Materials

Apart from buying a 2nd hand container, you can also find some great parts to build with for cheap or for free!

Check scrapyards, Craigslist, Garage sales etc. for parts you could potentially use in your build.

Finding old bits of steel, materials, or cut offs of timber can be a great way to reduce expenses. These materials can be used most commonly for non-structural components such as the exterior of your home, window frames, or curtains.

Get creative with your design by making use of these second-hand components. As they say – One man's trash is another man's treasure!

Chapter 13:
Foundation Types

The first step in building your container home is often overlooked in the planning process – the foundation type.

Choosing a solid foundation for your container home is vital, especially if you live in a location that is subject to harsh weather.

Your foundation needs will also depend on your structural needs, local government requirements, budget, and soil type. During this phase of the planning process it would be wise to consult with a structural engineer as foundation requirements will vary on a case-by-case basis.

If you are building on a soft soil type, a deeper foundation will obviously be required. But do not simply guess this on your own – consult a professional to evaluate your particular needs.

Concrete Piers

Concrete piers are the first type of foundation that you might like to consider.

These are usually the cheapest form of foundation and are quite a shallow form of foundation. They are basically concrete cubes that have steel bars inside of them to provide reinforcement.

These are the easiest form of foundation to do yourself, and they also have a few benefits.

They are cheap to acquire or create, and they physically lift your container home off of the ground, allowing for good ventilation, drainage, and protection against flooding.

Because they physically lift the container off of the ground, they are ideal to protect against condensation and rust to the underside of the container.

Slab On Grade

A slab on grade is your next type of foundation to consider.

This is more suited for larger container homes that stack containers and cover a large area.

This is a more time-consuming and more expensive form of foundation, however it is very stable and is excellent for soft soil types.

This form of foundation is also best suited to warmer climates where freezing isn't a concern. In colder climates the concrete slab can cause bad temperature losses.

Pile Foundations

Pile foundations are the most expensive form of foundation, and are used when the soil type is too weak to support concrete.

Piles are cylindrical steel poles that are driven deep into the ground. They provide a very stable foundation, but due to the depth they need to be driven are quite expensive and time-consuming to use.

Once the piles are in place they are usually capped with additional concrete.

For this type of foundation it is highly recommended to hire a contractor rather than attempting to do it yourself.

Conclusion

Thanks again for taking the time to read this book!

You should now have a lot of knowledge about shipping container homes, and be feeling excited to create your own!

Next, you simply need to begin brainstorming some design plans, consult with a few professionals, acquire your permits, and then get to work building! I wish you the best of luck with your shipping container home build!

If you enjoyed this book, please take the time to leave me a review on Amazon. I appreciate your honest feedback, and it really helps me to continue producing high quality books.